Scientists at Work

Geologists

Heather Hammonds

Smart Apple Media

This edition first published in 2005 in the United States of America by Smart Apple Media.

Smart Apple Media
1980 Lookout Drive
North Mankato
Minnesota 56003

Library of Congress Cataloging-in-Publication Data

Hammonds, Heather.
  Geologists / by Heather Hammonds.
  p. cm. — (Scientists at work)
  Includes index.
  ISBN 1-58340-543-7 (alk. paper)
  1. Geology—Vocational guidance—Juvenile literature. 2. Geologists—Juvenile literature.
  (1. Geologists. 2. Geology—Vocational guidance. 3. Vocational guidance.] I. Title.
  II. Scientists at work (Smart Apple Media)

QE34.H36 2004
551'.092—dc22   2003070431

First Edition
9 8 7 6 5 4 3 2 1

First published in 2004 by
MACMILLAN EDUCATION AUSTRALIA PTY LTD
627 Chapel Street, South Yarra, Australia, 3141

Associated companies and representatives throughout the world.

Copyright © Heather Hammonds 2004

Edited by Sally Woollett
Text and cover design by The Modern Art Production Group
Page layout by Raul Diche
Illustrations by Alan Laver, Shelly Communications Pty Ltd and Pat Kermode, Purple Rabbit Productions
Photo research by Jesmondene Senbergs
Printed in China

Acknowledgements

The author and the publisher are grateful to the following for permission to reproduce copyright material:

Cover photograph: Exposed rock at a road cutting, courtesy of © The Picture Source/Terry Oakley.

Armaco, p. 25; Maurice & Katia Krafft/Auscape, p. 20; Corbis, pp. 5, 12, 15 (bottom left), 21, 23; G. R. "Dick" Roberts Photo Library, pp. 9 (top), 13; Geoscience Australia, pp. 7 (all), 30; Great Southern Stock, pp. 14 (top left), 15 (top left), 19; Image Library, p. 15 (top right); Jiri Lochman/Lochman Transparencies, p. 14 (bottom left); Dennis Sarson/Lochman Transparencies, pp. 14 (top right, bottom right), 18; NASA, pp. 9 (bottom), 27 (all); Pelusey Photography, p. 8; Photodisc, pp. 15 (bottom right), 26; Saudi Arabia Embassy, p. 24; Sarah Saunders, p. 29; James King-Holmes/Science Photo Library, p. 15 (middle right); © The Picture Source/Terry Oakley, p. 28; U.S. Geological Survey, p. 4; Ruth Lathlean/World Images, p. 6; Leighton F. Young Jr., p. 22.

Author acknowledgements

Many thanks to Leighton F. Young Jr., Certified Petroleum Geologist, for kindly agreeing to be interviewed for this book; Craig Gumley, of Santos Australia, for his review of the manuscript; Dr. Alan Hildebrand, University of Calgary, Canada, for his help with pages 10 and 11; Professor Evan Leitch, University of Technology, Sydney, for his advice and review of the manuscript.

Please note

At the time of printing, the Internet addresses appearing in this book were correct. Owing to the dynamic nature of the Internet, however, we cannot guarantee that all these addresses will remain correct.

Contents

Glossary words
When you see a word printed in **bold**, you can look up its meaning in the glossary on page 31.

What is a geologist?

A geologist is a scientist who studies the Earth. Geologists study how the Earth's **crust** is formed and the materials it is made of. They collect samples of these materials, such as **minerals** and rocks, and examine them closely. Geologists learn a lot about the Earth by observing the landscape and rocks in different places. These places include mountains, canyons, cliffs, glaciers, rivers, and even the sea floor, deep underwater.

There are many areas of study within the science of geology, and geologists often specialize in one or more of them. Geologists travel to many different parts of the world. They discover new deposits of oil, gas, or other materials such as iron. They study very old rock formations and help uncover the hidden secrets of the Earth's past. The science of geology is one of discovery and excitement!

Geologists use many different machines and instruments to study the Earth. They may work in laboratories and offices, studying rock samples or maps. They may also work out in the field. There they study the landscape by flying over it in aircraft or walking through it, doing surveys and creating maps.

Scientists
working together

Geologists often work with other scientists, such as geophysicists. Geologists are **geoscientists**. Geophysicists are also geoscientists. Geophysicists use physics (the study of the physical world and how it works) to study the Earth's crust and areas deep beneath the surface of the Earth.

This geologist is working at Mount St. Helens in Washington.

The role of geologists

Geologists use their knowledge of the Earth's crust to play a very important role in the community.

Petroleum geologists look for places in the Earth's crust that are likely to contain oil and gas. Working with other scientists, they are able to direct mining companies to the best places to drill for these valuable fuels. Other exploration geologists identify sites where valuable materials such as gold or **iron ore** may be found.

Engineering geologists and structural geologists work with **engineers** on building projects, such as roads, tunnels, dams, and bridges.

Hydrogeologists work with other scientists to help manage water resources, by studying underground and surface water.

Environmental geologists work with other scientists to study pollution of the Earth's soil and water, and the effects of human activity on the landscape. They help work out the best ways to control and clean up pollution at different sites.

Some geologists study the age of rocks and rock formations, volcanoes, earthquakes, and the movement of **tectonic plates**. This information is very important to people who live on unstable parts of the Earth.

Geologists work in many different places, helping the public in many different ways.

Geology in the past

For thousands of years, people knew very little about the Earth and the materials it was made of.

Myths and legends

It was often thought that **landforms** such as mountains were the home of gods, or created by gods. In ancient Greek **mythology**, Mount Olympus, the highest mountain in Greece, was said to be the home of the gods. Myths and legends were also used to explain unusual landforms, such as the Giant's Causeway in Ireland. It is said to be the remains of a road between Ireland and Scotland, built by a giant.

Scientific study

The Greeks were among the first people to study the Earth's surface scientifically. Greek scientists and **philosophers** tried to explain how rocks, mountains, rivers, and oceans were formed and what they were made of. However, most of their explanations were wrong.

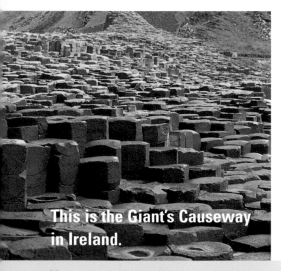

This is the Giant's Causeway in Ireland.

Key events in geology

300s B.C.	1669	1815	1896
Aristotle recognizes some areas of land were once covered by sea, and that fossils were once living creatures.	Nicolaus Steno discovers that layers of rock are deposited with the oldest on the bottom and youngest on top.	William Smith completes the first geological map of a whole country (England). He is the first person to use fossils to work out the age of rocks.	Radioactivity is discovered. In the early 1900s, several geologists and other scientists use radioactivity to prove the Earth is billions of years old.

	1620	1795	1830s and 1840s
	Frances Bacon notices how well the continents of Africa and South America would fit together (like a jigsaw puzzle).	James Hutton (sometimes called "the father of geology") writes *The Theory of the Earth*, a book that correctly describes how the Earth's crust gradually changes.	Louis Agassiz discovers that parts of Europe and North America were once covered by ice, which shaped the landscape.

Progress in geology

Geology advanced very little between ancient Greek times and the 1500s. Then scientists began to rely less on myths and legends as they studied the Earth's crust. They tried to work out the age of the Earth, and most believed it was only a few thousand years old!

Theories about the Earth's crust

Throughout the late 1700s and early 1800s, there were disagreements about how the Earth's crust formed:

- "Catastrophists" believed the Earth looked the way it did because sudden disasters, such as worldwide floods, had shaped it.
- "Neptunists" believed the Earth had once been covered by sea, and that all the Earth's crust had slowly formed on the sea floor. The land was uncovered as the sea dried up.
- "Plutonists" believed that many rocks were formed when **lava** from deep within the Earth came to the surface and cooled.

During the 1900s, new instruments and methods were used to learn much more about the Earth's crust. **Radiometric dating** showed that the Earth was billions of years old.

The formation of the Earth is no longer such a mystery. However, modern geologists are still uncovering the secrets of the Earth's past.

Fact Box

Geoscientists now know that there are three main types of rock:

Sedimentary rocks such as this sandstone form when pebbles and grains of sand and mud carried by water are left behind, and build up in one place, layer by layer.

Igneous rocks such as this granite form when **molten** rock from deep within the Earth comes to the surface and cools.

Metamorphic rocks such as this marble form when pressure or heat changes existing rocks.

1912
Alfred Wegener proposes the theory of continental drift and suggests all continents were once joined together.

1930s
Geologists discover large oil deposits in Saudi Arabia, a country that would become the world's largest oil producer.

1960s
Scientists propose the theory of plate tectonics.

1969–1972
United States astronauts collect rocks from the moon, enabling the geology of the moon to be studied.

1980
Geologist Walter Alvarez and his father Luis lead a team that discovers evidence of a comet or asteroid crash that caused a mass extinction 65 million years ago.

1990
Geologist and planetary scientist Dr. Alan Hildebrand leads a team that discovers the site of the comet or asteroid crash in Mexico.

1995
American scientists release the first complete map of the ocean floor, showing many new features of the Earth's crust.

Important discoveries

Many important discoveries have helped geologists and other scientists learn much about how the Earth has formed and the materials it is made of.

The age of rock layers

Some places show that the rock has formed in layers, or strata. In the late 1600s, a scientist named Nicolaus Steno studied rocks and fossils. He worked out that when rocks are deposited, or formed, the oldest layers are generally found at the bottom and the youngest at the top. This discovery is now called Steno's law of superposition.

You can easily see the rock strata in these cliff faces.

A fossil record

In the late 1700s and early 1800s, an English man named William Smith (1769–1839) traveled around England, surveying sites where new canals were to be built. As he studied rocks at canal sites, he noticed that layers of rock in different places contained the same types of fossils. Some types of fossils appeared in lower layers and others appeared in higher layers.

Smith worked out that different rocks from different places containing the same types of fossils were the same age.

Smith went on to create detailed **geological maps** of England and other parts of Britain. He was the first person in the world to create these types of maps.

An icy past

Ice ages are times in the Earth's history when the weather was much colder than it is at present. Enormous ice sheets, or glaciers, covered areas of North America and Europe during the last Ice Age, which ended about 10,000 years ago. Glaciers grow larger or smaller, depending on the warmth of the climate. As glaciers move they leave marks on the Earth's surface, such as deep valleys and piles of rocks.

Glaciers form deep valleys in the Earth's surface.

Until the 1830s, scientists did not know about ice ages and their effects on the Earth's surface. Then, in the 1830s and 1840s, a Swiss scientist named Louis Agassiz made a study of glaciers and rocks in Switzerland. Agassiz worked out that parts of Europe and North America were once covered by ice, which had shaped the landscape.

Moon rocks

For many years, geoscientists wondered about the geology of the moon. During the *Apollo* Space Program, astronauts traveled to the moon six times. Between 1969 and 1972, they collected 842 pounds (382 kg) of moon rocks and soil. Geologists and other geoscientists found that the rocks were between 3.2 and 4.6 billion years old, roughly the same age as the Earth. From these and other moon studies, many scientists believe that the moon formed when a large object such as another planet hit the Earth, blasting part of it into space.

Astronauts collected many rock samples from the moon during the *Apollo* Space Program.

Mass extinction

For many years, geologists and other scientists have known that there have been five **mass extinctions** during the Earth's history. The last mass extinction took place around 65 million years ago. At this time, around 70 percent of all life on Earth disappeared.

What could have caused this event? Read the student research notes to find out!

Fact Box

Geologists measure the age of rocks using the geologic time scale. This scale is mostly based on different layers of rock in the Earth's crust. The fossils within the rocks can give information about when the rocks were formed.

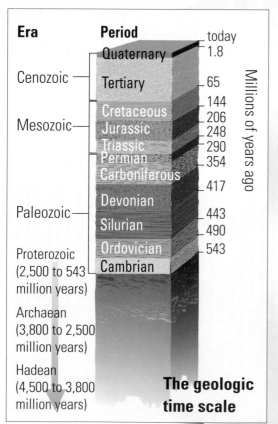

Era	Period	Millions of years ago
		today
Cenozoic	Quaternary	1.8
	Tertiary	65
	Cretaceous	144
Mesozoic	Jurassic	206
	Triassic	248
	Permian	290
	Carboniferous	354
Paleozoic	Devonian	417
	Silurian	443
	Ordovician	490
	Cambrian	543
Proterozoic (2,500 to 543 million years)		
Archaean (3,800 to 2,500 million years)		
Hadean (4,500 to 3,800 million years)		

The geologic time scale

Geology assignment notes: April 19

Geoscientists working for a Mexican oil company explored the Yucatán Peninsula, Mexico, in the 1950s and 1960s, searching for oil. They drilled out core samples of rock, looking for types of rocks that show oil may be present. No oil was found.

Notes: April 20

Glen Penfield, a petroleum geophysicist working for the Mexican oil company, surveyed the Yucatán Peninsula and the nearby sea floor in the late 1970s. Once again, he was searching for oil. Instead, the studies led Penfield and another scientist, Antonio Camargo, to believe a giant crater might lie beneath the ocean and part of the land. They wrote about their findings in 1981.

Notes: April 23

In 1980, a team of scientists led by geologist Walter Alvarez and his father, Luis, studied a thin layer of clay in the Earth's crust in Umbria, Italy. It forms the boundary between two time periods: the Cretaceous Period and the Tertiary Period. This boundary formed at the time of the last mass extinction.

The scientists found large amounts of iridium (a rare metal) in the clay.

Iridium is rare on Earth but common in asteroids and comets. They suggested that an enormous asteroid or comet crashed into the Earth. If this happened, huge amounts of dust would have been thrown into the **atmosphere**, darkening the sky for many months. Giant waves and earthquakes would have swept across the world. Most life on Earth could easily have been destroyed.

Notes: April 24

In 1990, geologist and planetary scientist Dr. Alan Hildebrand led a team, including Penfield and Camargo, that did further studies on the Yucatán Peninsula. They examined the core samples taken years before by the oil company, and found they contained materials formed by an asteroid or comet crash. They had finally found the site of this crash. A giant crater exists beneath the town of Puerto Chicxulub, Mexico. It was formed 65 million years ago and is now buried 3,280 feet (1 km) underground.

Notes: April 27

Today, most scientists agree that the asteroid or comet crash at Chicxulub probably caused the mass extinction. The Chicxulub crater is still being studied, to learn more about this event.

11

Training to be a geologist

Geologists work in a number of different fields, but they all need to learn certain common skills. Geologists become qualified by studying at college.

At school

Geology is a science, so high school students who want to become geologists need to study subjects such as physics, chemistry, math and English.

Subjects geologists use are:

- physics to understand how the Earth is formed
- chemistry to help them learn about the make-up of rocks
- math to help them sort and study information, usually done on computers
- English to communicate with other scientists, the media, and the public

A college degree

After finishing high school, people who want to become geologists study a Bachelor of Science degree at college. While studying for their degree, their main area of study is geology or geosciences.

Practical experience is an important part of learning geology.

Farther study

Geology students who have completed their bachelor's degree can do more study, called graduate study. Graduate students take advanced courses in geology, and do research in specific areas of geology. Graduate studies can take many years to complete.

After their final year of college, most students begin working as professional geologists.

At work

Geologists who have completed their degrees continue to learn more about their work throughout their careers. Many do field work in different places around the world. These experiences add to their knowledge of geology.

Most geologists work in teams, so it is important that geologists are good communicators and like to work with others. Newly qualified geologists usually begin with easier jobs within teams. Over time, as they gain more experience, they may become team leaders.

These geology students are gaining some practical experience.

On-the-job training

Geologists also continue to learn more by attending seminars and conferences on the latest discoveries in geology. They join geologists' associations, read books and magazines on their subject, and learn how to use new instruments.

Geologists are always learning!

Tools and instruments

Geologists use many different tools and instruments to do their work. They use tools and instruments in the field, in the laboratory, and in the office.

Compasses and clinometers

Combined compass and clinometer

Compasses are used in the field to measure the direction in which rock layers are running. This is called measuring "the strike." Compasses are also used when reading maps. Clinometers are used to measure the angle or slope of rock layers. This is called measuring "the dip." Compasses and clinometers are often combined as one instrument.

Drills

Drill

Drills are used to dig deep into the Earth and collect core samples of rock. The core samples are studied by geologists, geophysicists, and other geoscientists. Sometimes, the rock cores are hundreds of feet long.

Geological hammers and chisels

Geological hammer and chisels

Geological hammers and chisels are the geologist's most basic tools. They are used in the field to collect rock samples and examine different rocks.

Notebooks, pencils, and hand lenses

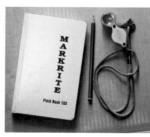

Notebook, pencil, and hand lens

These are very important tools, and during field trips they are carried at all times. Notebooks and pencils are used to record the location and descriptions of rock forms. Illustrations of rock formations can also be recorded. Hand lenses are small magnifying glasses that are used to examine rock specimens in the field.

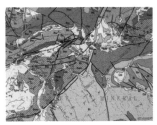
Geological map

Geological maps

Geological maps are color-coded maps that show the different types of rocks present on the Earth's surface at different places, and their ages.

Photographs

Geologists and other geoscientists use **aerial** photographs to help them create geological maps of different areas. Aerial photographs are also used to help find areas where oil, gas, or minerals may be present, and other sites of geological interest.

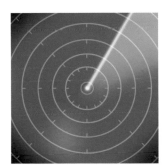
Radar screen

Radar

Radar stands for **RA**dio **D**etection **A**nd **R**anging. It is a system of sending and receiving radio waves, which bounce back when they hit objects and show what the objects look like. Geologists and other geoscientists use radar to study different landforms from the air. These landforms may be places such as mountains that are covered in clouds, and hard to reach from the ground.

Satellite

Satellites

Satellite images are used in similar ways to aerial photographs. They help locate areas where oil, gas, or minerals may be present, and other sites of geological interest.

Seismometer

Seismometers

Seismometers measure shock waves traveling through the Earth. They are used by geologists, **seismologists**, and other geoscientists to monitor earthquakes. Seismometers are also used to locate different types of rocks in the Earth's crust during explorations for oil and gas.

Computer

Computers and computer software

Computers are used to sort and process information gathered in the field or in the laboratory. Special computer programs are able to produce three-dimensional images of rock formations, helping geologists, geophysicists, and other geoscientists to visualize the Earth's crust.

Continents on the move

Dear George

My friend Sophia says that, long ago, the continents of the world were joined together. Then, over millions of years, they moved apart and ended up the way they are today. Is it true that continents move?

Carmen

Dear Carmen

It is true that continents move. This is called continental drift. Around 225 million years ago the land on the Earth probably existed as a single "supercontinent." Around 200 million years ago, this supercontinent split in two, forming Laurasia and Gondwanaland. By 135 million years ago, Laurasia and Gondwanaland began to break up and form the continents we know today.

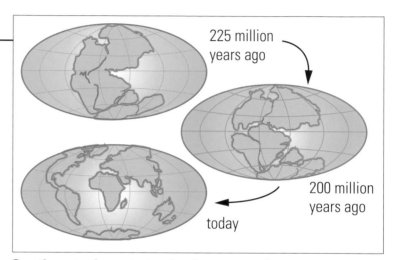

Continents do not stay in the same place.

Earth's continents are still slowly moving today, in a process called plate tectonics. The Earth's crust, and the solid part of the **mantle** directly below it, are made up of a number of tectonic plates. These plates move around very slowly on a layer of hot material in the mantle called the asthenosphere. Where tectonic plates meet, they slide under or past each other, or move apart. The continents on them then move too!

Your friendly geologist

George

The Earth has several different layers.

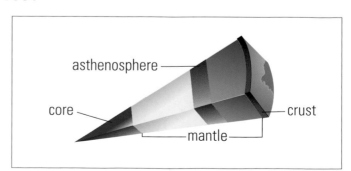

Dear George

Thank you for answering my question. Can you please tell me a little more about plate tectonics? When was the discovery that Earth's continents move about first made? And what instruments are used to study plate tectonics?

Carmen

Dear Carmen

It was hundreds of years ago that someone first noticed that the shape of some of the Earth's continents seemed to fit each other.

In the early 1900s, a scientist named Alfred Wegener developed the theory of continental drift. He studied rocks and fossils in Africa and South America, finding that they matched each other.

From the 1950s until now, the sea floors of the world have been studied and mapped using modern instruments. Huge mid-ocean ridges on the sea floors have been studied. It was discovered that the Earth's crust is being pulled apart at these ridges, as plates move apart. Molten rock then flows from faults in the crust, forming new crust. At other places on the sea floor, crust is being destroyed as one tectonic plate slides beneath another.

Farther studies of land and sea, using satellite tracking, seismometers, computers, and other modern instruments, are helping geoscientists learn more about plate tectonics.

Your friendly geologist

George

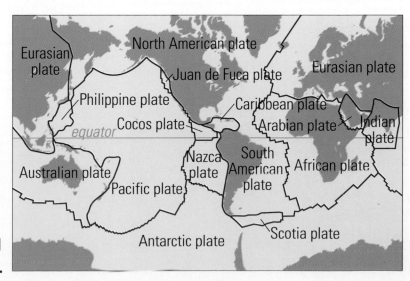

The Earth has several major tectonic plates.

Modern methods

Geologists work in the field, laboratories, and offices. They use the latest technology to help them study the Earth's crust.

In the field

Geologists often travel to remote places when taking part in field trips. Sometimes these places are only accessible by four-wheel-drive, or on foot. Several weeks at a time may be spent out in the field each year.

Geologists often work in teams with other geoscientists to perform geological surveys out in the field. Geological surveys are done for many reasons, such as locating oil, gas, and mineral resources. Test drills are sometimes set up at sites likely to contain these resources.

When out on field trips, geologists closely examine the landscape. They use aerial photographs and satellite information to help them find areas of interest. Modern instruments such as **global positioning systems** (GPS) are used to communicate with satellites and help pinpoint the exact positions of rock formations. Geologists also take photographs of rock formations, take samples of rocks, write lots of field notes, and make geological maps. Computers are used to store information and create maps.

This geologist is using portable GPS equipment.

Geologists, geophysicists, and other scientists also conduct **seismic** studies out in the field. They use seismometers to measure the speed of shock waves traveling through the Earth's crust. This tells them the types of rocks present and the shape of the layers. It also helps to pinpoint areas where oil and gas are likely to be found.

In the laboratory

Geologists work in laboratories alongside other scientists. They may examine core samples taken from drilling sites out in the field. The core samples show different layers of rock that lie beneath the ground.

Geologists also prepare samples of rocks, which can then be examined using special microscopes and other instruments. They study the rocks, and little fossils sometimes found in the rocks, to learn about the age of rocks and their composition.

In the office

Although geologists often prefer to work in the field or in laboratories, office work is a very important part of their job. Information gathered from field trips and laboratory work is brought together and studied in the office. Computers and computer programs are often used to create maps and images of the Earth's crust. Geological reports are made for governments, mining companies, building companies, and colleges. The office is a base for planning field trips, and for assembling and managing teams of other geoscientists.

Fact Box

Radiometric dating is a laboratory method used by geologists and other scientists to work out the age of rocks. The age of a rock can be found by studying the breakdown, or decay, of tiny amounts of different **radioactive** materials in it. The time that these materials take to break down shows the age of the rock. Radiometric dating is also used to estimate the age of other objects, such as ancient bones.

Laboratory work is an important part of a geologist's job.

19

Working on location

Geologists work in many different locations. Some geologists may travel in ships, studying the ocean floor. Others may work in hot and dangerous conditions at the edge of a volcano. From the icy, cold wastelands of Antarctica to the hot, dry deserts of outback Australia, geologists can be found at work.

Hawaiian volcanoes

The Hawaiian islands are a group of islands in the Pacific Ocean. The islands were created from volcanoes, over a "hot spot" in the Earth's crust. At hot spots, lava bursts through, forming volcanoes. Hawaii, the largest island in the group, is made up of five volcanoes. Two of these, Mauna Loa and Kilauea, are currently active. Hot lava flowing from the volcanoes is slowly increasing the size of Hawaii.

Geologists study volcanic activity in Hawaii. They study old and new lava flows, and collect samples of lava. They measure the advance of lava as it pours slowly from the volcanoes. They visit the edge of the volcanoes, monitoring the gases, rocks, and lava produced.

Studying volcanic activity in Hawaii and other places in the world helps geologists and other geoscientists to learn more about how the Earth's crust forms and the materials that lie beneath it. These scientists can also save lives by warning people about dangerous volcanic eruptions.

Working near a volcano can be hot and dangerous.

The amazing Andes

The Andes is one of the largest mountain ranges in the world. It stretches for more than 4,470 miles (7,200 km) along the length of South America. The Andes range was formed by the collision of two tectonic plates. The giant Pacific plate collided with the South American plate. The rock crumpled and buckled, and was pushed up. There are many volcanoes in the mountain range, and earthquakes often happen there.

The Andes mountain range is a place of great interest to geologists. Every year, geologists and other geoscientists travel to the Andes to study its towering snow-covered peaks, crumpled rock formations, volcanoes, and earthquakes.

Exploration geologists working for mining companies make field trips to the Andes, looking for minerals such as gold and tin. Some colleges organize field trips to the Andes for geology students, to help them learn about the special geology of these mountains.

Geologists working in the Andes often camp out in the mountains. Living conditions can be hard. In some places it is hot and sunny in the daytime and freezing cold at night!

Fact Box

The Andes range is still growing very slowly today, as the Pacific plate slips under the South American plate at a rate of about 4 inches (10 cm) a year.

The Andes mountain range is in South America.

Leighton F. Young Jr., geologist

Leighton F. Young Jr. has been a petroleum geologist for 43 years, working independently and running his own business for the last 37 years.

What does your job involve?

My job consists of performing **subsurface** geological studies, using electrical surveys recorded in previous oil wells, and also working with seismic data, which is recorded after noise is generated on the surface of the ground.

When did you first become interested in geology?

I became interested in geology during the summer of 1954, when I was working as a janitor in an office building in my home town of Houston, Texas. There were numerous geologists working there and, through them, I became interested in the profession. In retrospect, it was probably a nudge by God in the right direction. However, Dr. Ray Gutschick, a professor at the University of Notre Dame, created my love for geology.

Where did you study and what qualifications did you obtain?

I studied at the University of Notre Dame, Indiana, and graduated with a Bachelor of Science in geology, in 1959.

What was your first job as a geologist? Where have you worked since then?

I first worked for six years for a small but very active oil exploration company, Austral Oil Company. I gained a lot of experience with them and traveled, doing geological field work dealing with drill cutting from wells on the Texas–Mexico border to the North Dakota–Canadian border. After six years I went into business for myself. I have participated in the drilling of over 200 wells in the last 37 years.

What do you like most about your job?

I like the variety of subsurface geology within the various oil provinces of the world. There's always something new to learn. I also like the people in the oil business, really everything about the oil business!

What do you like least about your job?

The paperwork, deadlines, and people who don't do what they say they are going to do.

What are the difficulties and dangers of your job?

I have faced danger by being very near to wells which were touch-and-go as to whether they were about to blow out or not. I have also faced danger in the drilling of wells where poisonous gas is involved.

What was your most exciting geological project?

My most exciting project involved being one of the first geologists to go to the city of Baku in Azerbaijan in 1990, which was then part of the Soviet Union, to review their oil business and their geology.

What would you like to achieve in your job in the future?

In the future, I would like to retain the desire and ability to do what I am presently doing, that is, work as an independent petroleum geologist.

What advice would you give to young people interested in a career in geology?

Be sure you like the profession. Then pursue it, using your God-given talents!

Petroleum engineers sometimes work with geologists to test the oil pipes and drills of oil wells.

23

GEOLOGISTS AND AN OIL-RICH KINGDOM

Our energy-hungry world depends on oil. We use oil to make many different products, such as fuel and plastics. Without oil, our everyday lives would be very different. More than 60 years after oil was found in Saudi Arabia, we look back at the role of geologists in this discovery.

The oil-rich kingdom of Saudi Arabia has the largest reserves of oil in the world. Around 26 percent of the world's oil lies beneath this hot desert country and its seas. Saudi Arabia is also the world's largest oil **exporter**.

Before oil was discovered in Saudi Arabia, the way people lived there had changed very little for thousands of years. The discovery of oil brought great riches to the country.

Today, the people of Saudi Arabia enjoy a modern, wealthy lifestyle with excellent schools, hospitals, and other community services.

What part did geologists play in changing Saudi Arabia forever?

Fact Box

Oil is a **fossil fuel**. Oil is found underground, in certain types of rock formations. Geologists and geophysicists play important roles in the search for oil. They conduct surveys to identify sites where oil may be found and work at test drilling sites, searching for oil.

This oil field, "Rastanur," is the largest oil field in Saudi Arabia.

This geological exploration team worked in Saudia Arabia in 1936.

In 1933, the King of Saudi Arabia gave permission to an American company to explore eastern parts of the country, in search of oil. **Oil reserves** had been found in surrounding countries, but no **commercial** oil reserves had been discovered in Saudi Arabia itself. Many people thought there were none.

A small team of young American geologists traveled to Saudi Arabia to begin the search. The geologists worked with local guides, traveling through hostile deserts. They camped out in the wilderness. They endured hot desert days where the temperatures could reach above 113 °F (45 °C). Water was scarce and often salty, and almost undrinkable. Fierce sand and dust storms sometimes swept the land.

The geologists studied the landscape, made maps, and drilled test wells. At first they had no luck and found no commercial oil reserves. Still they kept looking, across the huge, hot country. Then, more than four years after the search had begun, they found what they were looking for, a huge reservoir of oil!

More oil reserves were discovered and, over time, Saudi Arabia became the world's largest oil producer.

Fact Box

Geologists have also found reserves of valuable minerals in Saudi Arabia. Gold, silver, copper, and lead are just a few of the riches discovered beneath the deserts.

Geology in the future

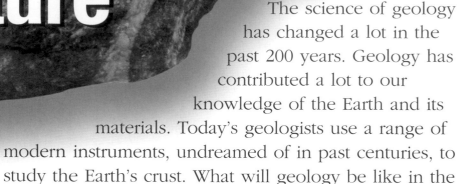

The science of geology has changed a lot in the past 200 years. Geology has contributed a lot to our knowledge of the Earth and its materials. Today's geologists use a range of modern instruments, undreamed of in past centuries, to study the Earth's crust. What will geology be like in the future?

Mining and energy

Every day, the world uses enormous amounts of materials from the Earth. Iron is mined and used to make steel. Copper, tin, and lead are just a few of the other materials that are mined and made into things we use. Fossil fuels such as oil, gas, and coal are also used in huge quantities to provide the world with fuel, plastics, and other products.

Minerals and fossil fuels are created naturally over millions of years. They are **non-renewable resources**. The role of exploration geologists and other geoscientists in locating new reserves will become more important as these resources become harder to find.

Fact Box

Today's technology is helping geologists and other geoscientists to locate reserves of minerals and fossil fuels that could never have been found 50 years ago. Satellites, GPS units, powerful computers, and other modern scientific instruments will continue to help future geologists in their search for resources.

We dig a huge amount of fossil fuels from the ground.

Geologists and the environment

There are currently more than 6.2 billion people on Earth, and the world's population is slowly increasing. This increase means that work in some areas of geology will become more important.

As a population grows, it needs more water. In some places, water is very scarce. Geologists are already working to find sources of underground water. In the future, this search will become more important because world usage of water will increase.

Environmental geologists study such things as soil erosion, disposal of waste, and pollution. These problems can be harder to solve when the population is increasing. In the future, more environmental geologists will be needed to help manage the effects of our activities on the environment.

This photograph of the Atlantic coast of Western Sahara in Africa was taken from space. The red lines are sand dunes and the gray-brown areas represent coastal salt flats.

Other planets

Planetary scientists study the surfaces of planets and other objects in our solar system using information collected by space probes and telescopes, or from meteorites that fall to Earth. Planetary scientists and geologists of the distant future may travel to the moon, asteroids, and Mars. They may use their skills to help set up bases, or locate valuable minerals.

One of the *Viking* landers

Fact Box

Geologists of the future may travel to Mars, but the first "geologists" on Mars were machines. In 1976, the American *Viking* landers studied soil samples and set up seismometers, transmitting their findings back to Earth.

Get involved in geology

You can get involved in geology in your own neighborhood. Here are some fun activities you might like to try.

Explore the geology of your area

You will need:
- an adult helper
- notebook and pen
- hard hat and safety glasses
- hand lens or magnifying glass
- hammer (a geological one is best, but a regular one will also work)
- plastic bags

What to do:
1 Ask an adult to help you find a place where rock is **exposed**, such as a road cutting.
2 Write the location you are visiting in your notebook. Can you see the rock strata, or layers? Using your hand lens, look closely at the exposed rock. Write down what you see.
3 Collect some rock samples and put them in plastic bags. Write the date and location on the bags.

Safety
! Some road cuttings, cliffs, and embankments are extremely dangerous, as rockfalls may occur. Always have an adult's help on a field trip and only visit places that are known to be safe.
! Always wear a hard hat when standing near cliffs or steep embankments.
! Never climb cliffs or steep embankments without expert help.
! Always wear safety glasses when using a hammer.
! Always ask before collecting rock samples from private land.

Rock display

You can display the rocks you collect on field trips.

You will need:

- small rocks, collected on field trips
- book on rocks and minerals (available at most libraries)
- shallow wooden or cardboard box
- several thin cardboard strips
- white paint pen
- sticky labels and a pen

What to do:

1 Identify your rock samples. Remember that there are three main types of rock: sedimentary rocks, igneous rocks, and metamorphic rocks. However, there are many different rocks within these categories. There are also many types of minerals. A book on rocks and minerals will help you identify exactly what samples you have collected.

2 Gently wash the rock samples in water, so they will look their best.

3 Place the strips of cardboard into the shallow box, making several small compartments of equal size.

4 Place a small number on the "bottom" of each rock, using the paint pen.

5 Write a sticky label for each rock. You will need to write the rock type, number, and where it was found. Then stick each label in a compartment of the box.

6 Place the numbered rocks in each compartment, in their correct places. Now you can display your collection, for everyone to see!

More to do

Get your whole class involved in geology!

- Take a class geological field trip.

- Publish a report in your school newsletter on the geology in your area.

- Ask a geologist to give a talk to your class.

Check it out!

Geology is an exciting science. You can learn more about geology, and the jobs of geologists and other geoscientists, by checking out some of these places and Web sites.

Government agencies

Most countries have a national geoscience agency, and many states do too. You can learn more about the science of geology by contacting them. Most of these agencies have informative and interesting websites.

United States Geological Survey   http://geology.usgs.gov/index.shtml

California Geological Survey   http://www.consrv.ca.gov/CGS/index.htm

Alaska Geological and Geophysical Survey   http://wwwdggs.dnr.state.ak.us/

Geology clubs and associations

There are many clubs and associations around the world for those who are interested in geology. Some are for professional geologists, but others are for anyone who is interested in the subject.

Web sites

Geological Society of America   http://www.geosociety.org/

International Union of Geological Scientists   http://www.iugs.org/

The Rock'n Science Club   http://sciencerocks.usgs.gov/index2.htm

Glossary

aerial   in the air

atmosphere   the gases that surround a planet

commercial   something that money can be made from, that is profitable

crust   the outermost part of the Earth that lies above the mantle

engineers   professional people with college degrees who use science to build or design different types of machines and instruments

exporter   a person or company who sends goods or resources to other countries

exposed   uncovered and able to be seen

fossil fuel   a fuel such as coal, oil, or gas, formed from the remains of plants and animals that lived millions of years ago

fossilized   turned into a fossil. Fossils are the remains of plants or animals that lived long ago – usually millions of years ago.

geological maps   color-coded maps that show the geology of an area – the different types of rocks and landforms in an area

geoscientists   scientists who study the Earth and the materials it is made of

global positioning systems (GPS)   systems that use satellites to locate the position of objects on Earth to within a few feet

iron ore   the raw material that steel is made from

landforms   features that make up the landscape, such as mountains, canyons, cliffs, and glaciers

lava   hot, liquid rock from deep within the Earth

mantle   a part of the Earth beneath the crust that is around 1,800 miles (2,900 km) thick and surrounds the innermost part of the Earth, the core

mass extinctions   the death of large numbers of living things, all at once

minerals   naturally occurring materials that are not formed from animals or plants. Rocks are formed from one or more types of minerals.

molten   melted, usually in a liquid state

mythology   traditional stories of fiction, usually about imaginary people or creatures

non-renewable resources   materials used by people which cannot be renewed or replaced quickly

oil reserves   stores of oil, such as oil fields or oil traps, which are places where oil has collected

philosophers   people who study philosophy, which is the study of all knowledge, wisdom, and science

radioactive   giving off radiation (a form of energy)

radiometric dating   a laboratory technique used by geologists and other scientists to work out the age of rocks, by studying the breakdown of tiny amounts of radioactive materials in them

seismic   relating to vibrations in the Earth, such as those caused by earthquakes

seismologists   scientists who study vibrations in the Earth (called seismic waves), whether they are caused by earthquakes or created by machines, such as when geoscientists are searching for oil

subsurface   beneath the Earth's surface

tectonic plates   large parts of the Earth's crust and mantle that move about very slowly, on a layer of hot material

Index